Nightmare Bugs!

Bedbugs

By Natalie Humphrey

Gareth Stevens Publishing

Hot Topics

Please visit our website, www.garethstevens.com. For a free color catalog of all our high-quality books, call toll free 1-800-542-2595 or fax 1-877-542-2596.

Library of Congress Cataloging-in-Publication Data

Names: Humphrey, Natalie, author.
Title: Bedbugs / Natalie Humphrey.
Description: Buffalo, NY : Gareth Stevens Publishing, [2025] | Series: Nightmare bugs! | Includes index.
Identifiers: LCCN 2023042319 | ISBN 9781538292099 (library binding) | ISBN 9781538292082 (paperback) | ISBN 9781538292105 (ebook)
Subjects: LCSH: Bedbugs–Juvenile literature.
Classification: LCC QL523.C6 H86 2025 | DDC 595.7/54–dc23/eng/20231108
LC record available at https://lccn.loc.gov/2023042319

First Edition

Published in 2025 by
Gareth Stevens Publishing
2544 Clinton St
Buffalo, NY 14224

Designer: Andrea Davison-Bartolotta
Editor: Natalie Humphrey

Photo credits: Cover, p. 13 Georgy Dzyura/Shutterstock.com; series art (texture) Video_Stock _Production/Shutterstock.com; series art (lines) Hananta S/ Shutterstock.com; series art (sign) Mr Doomits/Shutterstock.com; series art (trees) Wilqkuku/Shutterstock.com; p. 5 Jay Ondreicka/Shutterstock.com; p. 7 Vector Tradition/Shutterstock.com; p. 9 CDC/Janice Haney Carr; p. 10 7th Son Studio/ Shutterstock.com; p. 11 juerginho/Shutterstock.com; p. 15 Akos Nagy/ Shutterstock.com; pp. 17, 25 (bottom) simon berenyi/Shutterstock.com; p. 19 Dmitrii Erekhinskii/Shutterstock.com; pp. 21, 23, 27 whitejellybeans/Shutterstock.com; p. 25 (top) Crystal Eye Studio/Shutterstock.com; p. 29 Penyushkina/Shutterstock.com; p. 30 (bug) D. Kucharski K. Kucharska/Shutterstock.com; p. 30 (stamp) Miloje/ Shutterstock.com.

Printed in the United States of America

CPSIA compliance information: Batch #CS25GS: For further information contact Gareth Stevens, New York, New York at 1-800-542-2595.

CONTENTS

BEDBUGS!

Just saying the word "bedbug" can make a person itchy! This nightmare bug makes its home in people's beds around the world. But this **parasite** does more than just live alongside humans. It drinks human blood!

Terrible Truths

Bedbugs will drink blood from any warm-blooded animal, but human blood is their favorite food!

Bedbug BODIES

Bedbugs are insects, or small animals with six legs and three body parts. An adult bedbug is only 0.2 to 0.3 inch (5 to 7 mm) long! Bedbugs are flat and oval shaped. Their bodies are brown or reddish.

Terrible Truths

Adult bedbugs don't have wings but do have wing pads! These pads are where wings would have grown if bedbugs had them.

Bedbug Body

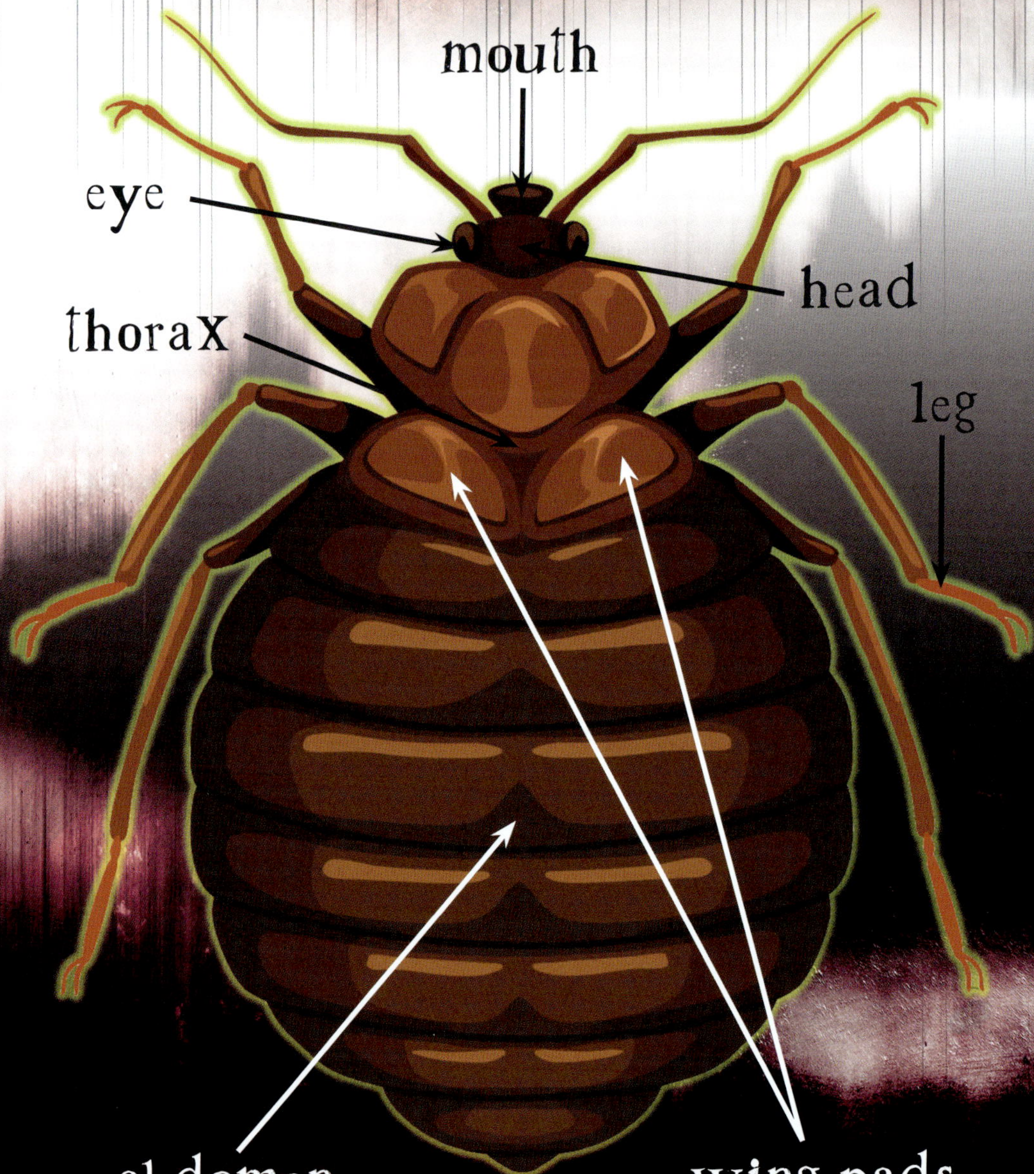

Bug BITES

Bedbugs already look gross, but their mouth is straight out of a nightmare! A bedbug's mouth has a part like a drinking straw. This tube is called a proboscis (proh-BAH-sihs). A bedbug's proboscis can **pierce** human skin and suck blood.

Terrible Truths

Bedbugs usually bite people more than once. They'll bite any skin that is exposed, or not covered.

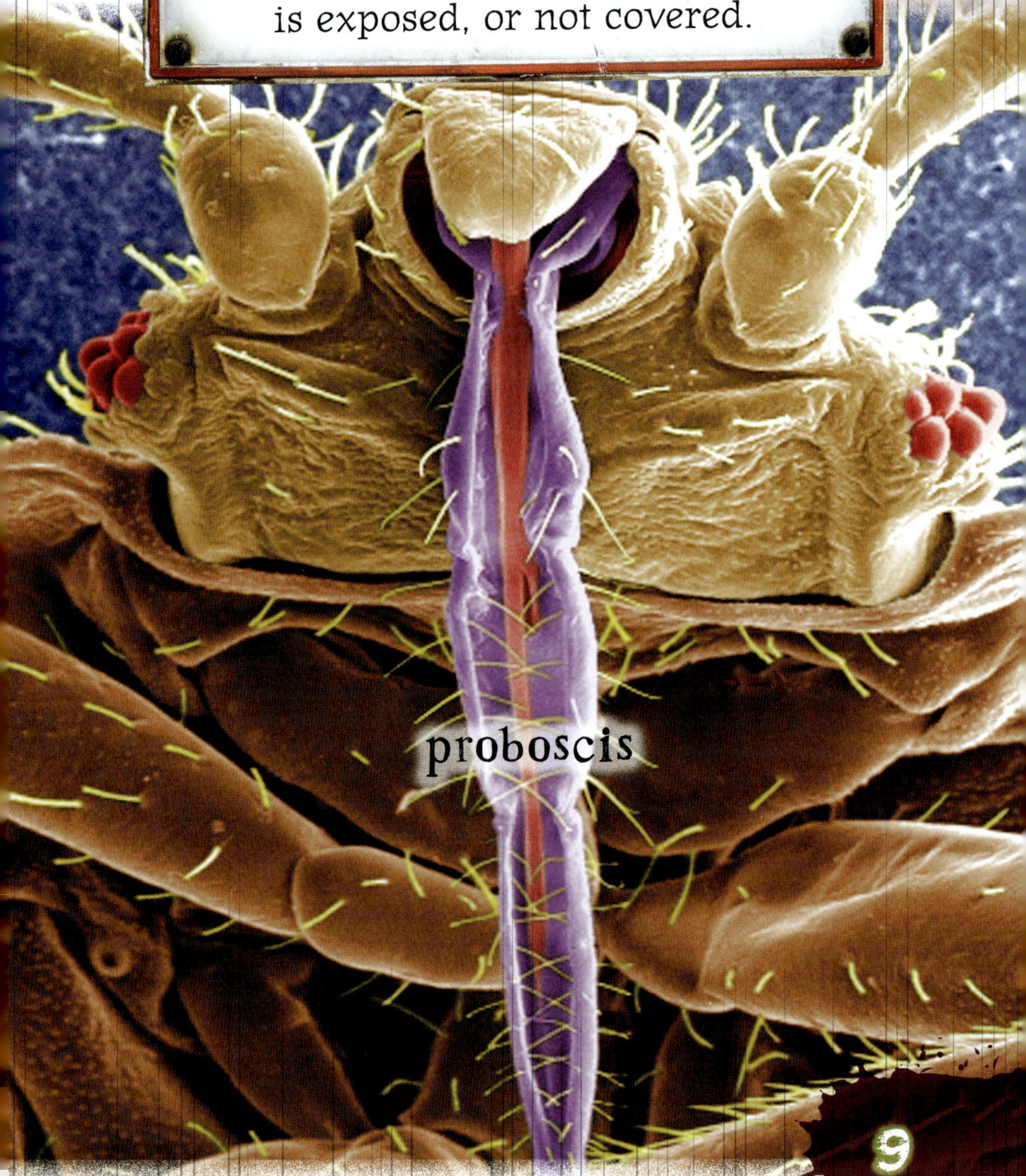

Bedbug bites can be different from person to person. Some people won't notice a bedbug has bitten them. For others, bedbug bites can hurt. Bedbug bites can be itchy. The bites are usually small, red dots but can swell, or grow, much larger!

Terrible Truths

A bedbug bite is filled with saliva. Saliva is the watery matter animals make in their mouths to break down food. Some people are **allergic** to the saliva in bedbug bites.

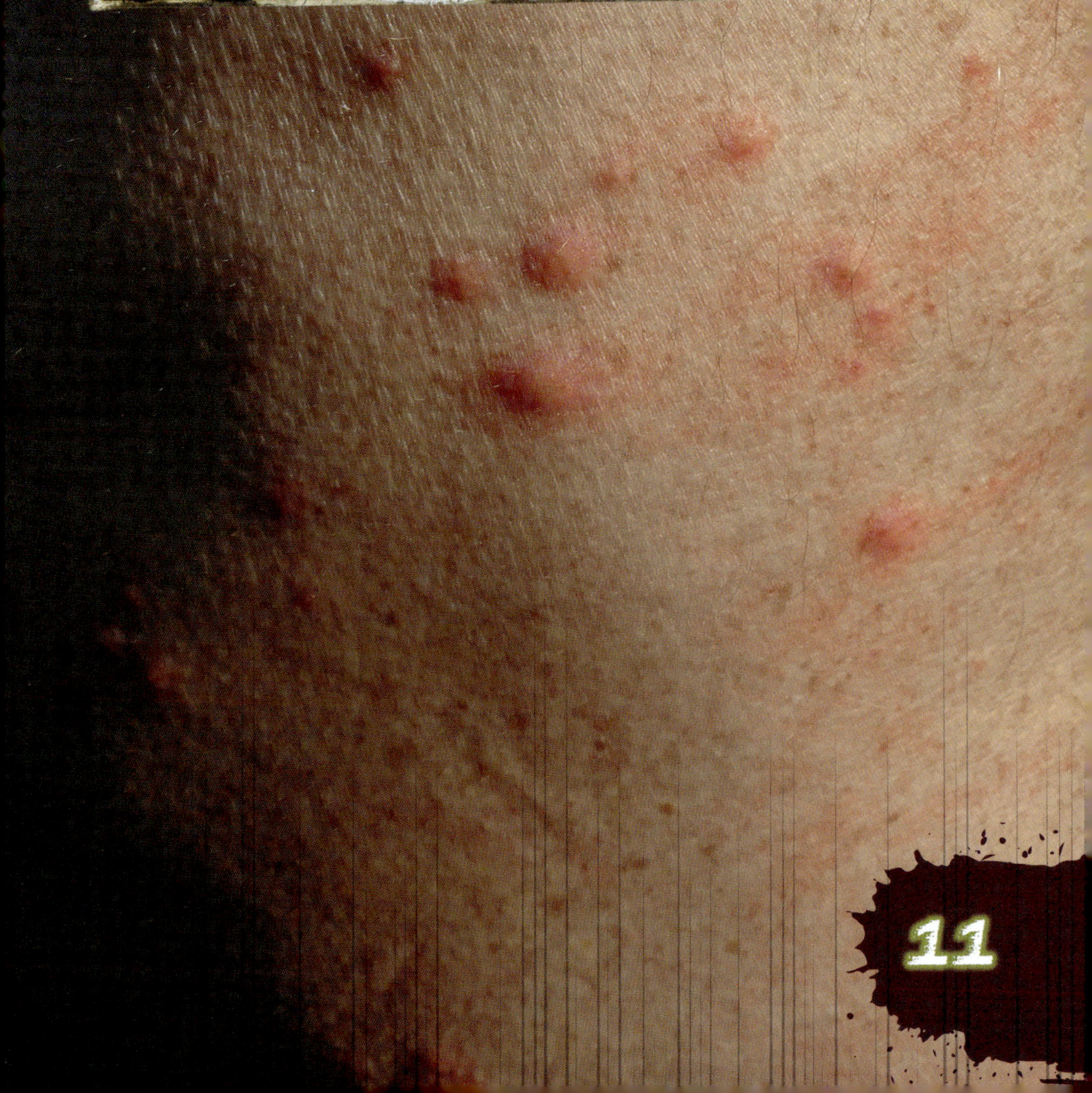

Always NEARBY

Bedbugs live close to humans. They can be found in dark places where they can easily hide. Bedbugs like to live in beds, but can also be found in bed **frames**, inside couches, and in blankets. Their hiding spots usually aren't more than about 8 feet (2.4 m) from humans.

Terrible Truths

Bedbugs can travel 100 feet (30.5 m) or more in just one hour!

Nighttime SNACK

Bedbugs usually eat at night when they won't get caught. They can eat a lot for their size. One bedbug can eat six times its body weight in blood! Bedbugs will usually feed for around 3 to 10 minutes.

Terrible Truths

Bedbugs don't have to eat all the time! A bedbug can **survive** for around 400 days without eating.

Bedbugs EVERYWHERE!

Bedbugs can be found in every country around the world. If there are people, bedbugs can be found there. There are many different species, or kinds, of bedbugs. Each species is suited to the **climate** where it lives.

Terrible Truths

The common bedbug can be found in North America, Europe, and Central Asia.

Spreading FAST

Bedbugs are already a nightmare, but their spread makes them a little scarier. If a person visits a place that has bedbugs, the bugs crawl into their bag and go for a ride! Because bedbugs are so small, it's easy to miss them.

Terrible Truths

People used to think that bedbugs only lived in dirty or rundown places. But bedbugs can survive anywhere if there are enough people to bite!

Spotting BEDBUGS

Because bedbugs are so hard to see, it might be tough to know if you have them or not. Checking for them in places they like to hide is one way to find them. Another way is to look in your bed for bedbug poop!

Terrible Truths

Bedbug poop is gross! It can look like tiny rusty red or brown spots.

Too Many EGGS

Female bedbugs are larger than male bedbugs. They usually lay around five eggs in one day. During her lifetime, a female bedbug may lay up to 500 eggs! These eggs are white and only around 0.1 inch (2.5 mm) long.

Terrible Truths

Bedbugs usually live four to six months, but some have lived for a whole year!

Baby BEDBUGS

Bedbug eggs hatch in around 4 to 10 days. The baby bedbugs eat right away. They look much like adult bedbugs. They are clear and very small. To grow into adults, a bedbug will molt. This means the bedbug sheds its skin!

Terrible Truths

Bedbugs molt five different times before they become adults.

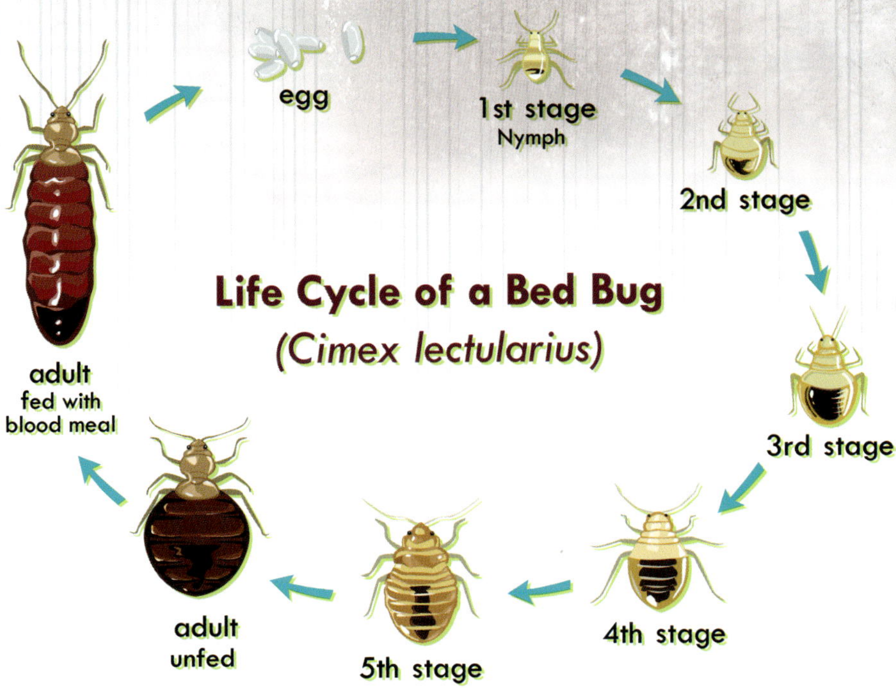
Life Cycle of a Bed Bug
(Cimex lectularius)
egg
1st stage
Nymph
2nd stage
3rd stage
4th stage
5th stage
adult
unfed
adult
fed with
blood meal

Bye BEDBUGS!

Bedbugs are hard to get rid of. **Exterminators** might need to be called. Exterminators use **pesticides** to get rid of bedbugs. If you find a bite you think might be from a bedbug, or see a bedbug, tell an adult!

Terrible Truths

Some bedbugs are resistant to normal pesticides. This means the bedbug can still live even after being sprayed.

Preventing, or stopping, bedbugs can be easy. Since they can only walk from place to place, the only way to get bedbugs is to visit a place that has them already. When you visit a new place, always check for bedbugs!

Terrible Truths

After traveling, be sure to check your clothes and suitcase for any bedbugs that caught a ride. You may want to wash your clothes too just in case there's a bedbug or an egg you can't see!

Tiny Terrors

BEDBUGS

Size:	0.2 to 0.3 inch (5 to 7 mm); around the size of an apple seed
Appearance:	brown or reddish with a flat body
Life span:	between four to six months but can live up to one year
Habitat:	around the world
Diet:	blood from animals, mostly humans
Nightmare Fact:	Bedbugs will bite a human more than once each time they eat!

FOR MORE INFORMATION

BOOKS

Pakpour, Nazzy. *Please Don't Bite Me*. London, England: Flying Eye Books, 2023.

Sanchez, Anita. *Itch!* New York, NY: Clarion Books, 2022.

WEBSITES

AZ Animals
www.a-z-animals.com/animals/bed-bugs/
Check out more photos of bedbugs and learn more about them.

Pest World for Kids: Bed Bugs
www.pestworldforkids.org/pest-guide/bed-bugs/
Learn more facts about bedbugs and how to prevent them.

Publisher's note to educators and parents: Our editors have carefully reviewed these websites to ensure that they are suitable for students. Many websites change frequently, however, and we cannot guarantee that a site's future contents will continue to meet our high standards of quality and educational value. Be advised that students should be closely supervised whenever they access the internet.

GLOSSARY

allergic: Relating to having an allergy, which is a medical condition where something usually harmless such as dust or pollen causes someone to become sick.

climate: The average weather conditions of a place over a period of time.

exterminator: Someone who gets rid of pests.

frame: Something that holds up or gives shape to something else.

parasite: A living thing that lives in, on, or with another living thing and often harms it.

pesticide: Something used to kill pests, such as bugs.

pierce: To make a hole through.

survive: To live through something.

INDEX